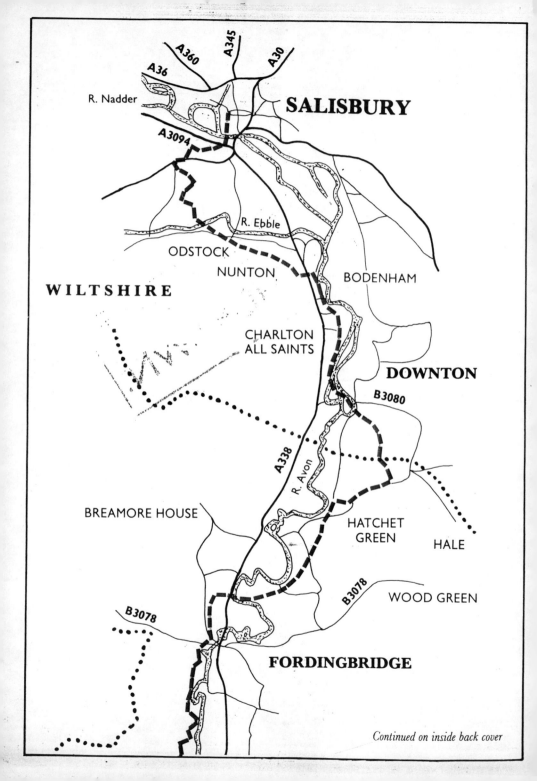

Continued on inside back cover

THE
AVON VALLEY PATH

and other walks
near the
Hampshire Avon

by
Members of the New Forest Group of the
Ramblers' Association and edited by
Marjorie Kerr

First published May 1994

ISBN 0-86146-088X

Published by Paul Cave Publications Ltd.,
74 Bedford Place, Southampton

£3.50

Printed by Brown & Son, Crowe Arch Lane, Ringwood, Hants. Tel: (0425) 476133

MAP READING

It is recommended that walkers use Ordnance Survey maps and carry a compass. Maps required are:

OS Landranger sheet 184 — 'Salisbury and the Plain' *and*

OS Landranger sheet 195 — 'Bournemouth and Purbeck' *or*

OS Leisure Map sheet 22 — 'The New Forest'.

The starting point of each walk is given with a **GRID REFERENCE** (GR). For those not used to an Ordnance Survey map, the following information is given.

The GR should be read as two sets of three figures.

The first two refer to the numbers across the top and bottom of the map. Look for the vertical line at these figures, then imagine that the section between this and the next higher number is divided into ten strips. The third figure indicates the strip.

The second set of three figures refers in a similar manner to the horizontal lines and the numbers are shown on either side of the map. Now look at the diagram below.

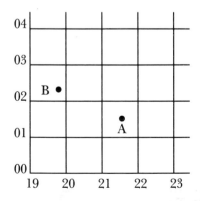

A would be at GR 215015
B would be at GR 199022

FOREWORD

The Avon Valley Path was the brainchild of a group of walkers from the Ringwood and Fordingbridge Footpath Society, supported by members of the New Forest Group of the Ramblers' Association. The idea was welcomed by Hampshire County Council's Rights of Way Manager, Colin Piper, and backed by officers from the neighbouring counties of Wiltshire and Dorset.

It seemed appropriate to start from Salisbury Cathedral, walking in a mainly southerly direction to reach Christchurch Priory at the confluence of the Rivers Avon and Stour, just before they reach the coast. The route passes through a variety of landscapes, including areas that are designated Sites of Special Scientific Interest and Environmentally Sensitive Areas. At certain times of year many wild flowers will delight the eye, and the ear will rejoice at the cries of birds. English Nature has described the River Avon as having 'a greater range of habitat diversity and more diverse flora and fauna than any other chalk river in Britain'.

The path totals 34 miles, so could be walked in two days by those who relish covering a long mileage each day. In this book we have broken down the route into seven easy stages which can be taken separately, joined into lengths to suit the individual or, in some instances, made into a circular walk using one of the additional routes.

The path does not keep to the banks of the Avon as private ownership of land and private fishing rights would not permit this. It keeps to existing rights of way and, apart from one short track near Avon Tyrell, no new paths were created. However, the river is never far away and is crossed and recrossed several times. There are also crossings of the main road from Salisbury to Ringwood — the A338 — and of the B3347 between Ringwood and Christchurch. This makes it easy to complete one or two sections at a time and return by bus. The Wilts and Dorset service X3 runs between Salisbury, Fordingbridge and Ringwood approximately every hour on weekdays.

When long-distance paths are designed there is a danger that other rights of way in their vicinity may become neglected. In order to avoid this, and because there are many other delightful paths to explore in or near the Avon Valley, we have provided seven additional walks. Some offer a return route from a section of the AVP, creating a circular walk, while others are complete in themselves. All have been carefully researched by members of the New Forest RA Group.

There are, of course, many interesting places to explore along the way, so do not hurry to complete the AVP without allowing time to discover and enjoy the little towns and villages that you pass through.

Marjorie A. Kerr

The stream near Sopley on the Avon Valley Path.

CONTENTS

The Avon Valley Path
Section   **Page No.**

Walks in the Avon Valley

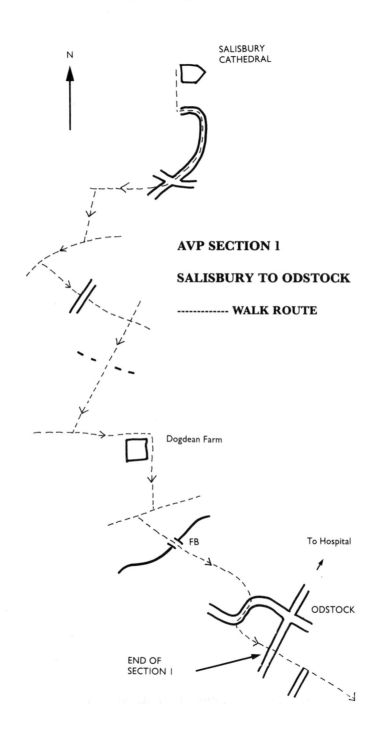

SALISBURY
CATHEDRAL

N

AVP SECTION 1

SALISBURY TO ODSTOCK

------------ **WALK ROUTE**

Dogdean Farm

FB

To Hospital

ODSTOCK

END OF
SECTION 1

SECTION 1 — SALISBURY TO ODSTOCK — 4 miles
Contributed by Erica and John Bamford

Salisbury can be reached by bus, coach or train from many parts of the country.

There are ample car parks, well signposted, including the Central Car Park (long-term parking) reached from the ring road between Castle Road and Wilton Road roundabouts.

Those who do not know Salisbury will, no doubt, wish to spend time exploring this fascinating city, either before starting on the walk or on arriving back here. The Cathedral is usually the major attraction but there are many other buildings of historical interest and it is worthwhile visiting the Information Centre for details of these.

The walk starts from the Cathedral Close (GR 142295) and soon crosses the River Avon by the Old Harnham Bridge (crossed by Tess and Angel on their way to Stonehenge at the end of *Tess of the D'Urbevilles*). It continues up to Bishop's Walk, which originally afforded views of the Cathedral, then goes over downland before crossing the River Ebble and its water meadows to reach the village of Odstock.

The Route

From the west front of the Cathedral turn south (right when facing the Cathedral) to follow the gravel track to Harnham Gate leading out of the Close. Follow the road (now east) to a junction, then turn right (south) to Old Harnham Bridge. Immediately after crossing the Bridge, turn right (south-west) along Harnham Road, passing the picturesque 'Rose and Crown Hotel'. On reaching the junction with New Harnham Road, cross it and turn left immediately (south-west) to go up Old Blandford Road.

In 200 yards, turn right into the entrance of Grasmere Close then immediately left onto the lower path (west) with the AVP signpost. In 50 yards take the steps on the left (south) to reach Bishop's Walk which contours along the hillside with a wooded area below and gardens above. Ignore all paths going downhill and the steps and a path on the left. Continue, passing the stone to Bishop Wordsworth, for a quarter of a mile. Where there is a wooden half fence across the path, turn left (south) through a 'squeeze' stile.

Continue on this path, with gardens on the left and fields on the right for another quarter of a mile. On reaching a crossing track, turn right (west) going under power lines. On reaching a hardcore track, turn left (south-east) to reach the A354 in 100 yards.

Cross this road and take the track ahead (south-east) for a third of a mile to where a path crosses the track. Turn right (south-west), over a stile and follow the path down to the Dogdean Farm road. Turn left (east) onto it and follow it to the end of the farm buildings.

(NB The section from Harnham Hill to Dogdean Farm could be affected by the proposed Salisbury Southern By pass.)

Turn right (south) and follow a track towards the River Ebble. On reaching a wide grassy cross track, go right and then immediately cross the stile on the left into the field. Bear left (south-east) diagonally across the field, go through into the next field and in a few yards cross two footbridges over the Ebble. The path goes through a short, uncultivated area by the side of the river and crosses a stile into a field. Turn left (east) and go along the field, under power lines to a gate ahead. Go through this, then immediately through another gate on the right leading into the next field. Follow the fence to the left, continuing in an easterly direction to a gate and stile onto the road at the start of Odstock.

Turn right (south) for 20 yards to the bend in the road and go straight ahead through a gate/stile. Turn left (east) in 20 yards, round the corner of the fence and continue, crossing the stile into the football field. This leads into a street which reaches a crossing road. The 'Yew Tree Inn' is a short distance along the road on the left, but the AVP continues straight ahead (see next section).

Walkers finishing here will find the bus stop (service X3) along the road on the left. If there is not a convenient bus from the village, there is a frequent service from the Hospital, two-thirds of a mile to the north.

Below: The opening of the Avon Valley Path at Castle Hill.

SECTION 2 — ODSTOCK TO DOWNTON — 4 miles
Contributed by Cliff Roffey

If arriving in Odstock by car there is off-road parking for about a dozen vehicles on the left-hand side of the approach road from the A338, a few yards past the village school. The crossroads are about 200 yards further along the same road.

Those travelling by bus (service X3) should alight at Odstock crossroads, but note that only every other bus between Salisbury and Fordingbridge travels via Odstock. However, the village is only about half a mile from the A338 where there is a bus stop at the Odstock turn-off.

From the crossroads walk past the 'Yew Tree Inn' and after a few yards turn left to join the signposted AVP.

This section of the AVP starts in Odstock village (GR 146262). The walk passes through the attractive village of Charlton All Saints and across the water meadows to the north of Downton.

The Route
Follow the footpath alongside a cottage garden to reach and cross a stile. Bear right across a field to a five-barred gate in the right-hand corner. Go through this and two more gates in quick succession. Bear right (south-east) across an open field, passing to the left of a telephone pole and heading towards a small clump of oak trees on the far side. Climb a stile and follow a barbed wire fence and sparse hedge on the left to a metal six-barred gate. Bear left onto a tarmac road and after about 200 yards, as the road bends left, go straight ahead onto a farm road. Follow this for about half a mile, cross a stile and bear right (south) under a power line, following the edge of the field. Cross another stile, turn sharp left and walk towards the A338 (Salisbury road).

Cross the road to a clearly signposted path (AVP). Climb two stiles into a field and head south-east to a five-barred gate in the right-hand corner. There turn right onto a country lane and follow this to a T-junction. Bear left over a stile on the right-hand side of a metal farm gate. Walk alongside the farm entrance road to cross a second stile and head towards the right-hand corner of an open field. Cross two further stiles in quick succession leading onto a farm road and turn right. After 100 yards go through a kissing gate and bear right across the open field in the broad direction of a church. Approaching the far side of the field an AVP sign should be seen to the right of the church. Cross the stile at the sign, turn left on the metalled road and pass the church. Turn right at Chapel Lane and follow the road through Charlton All Saints.

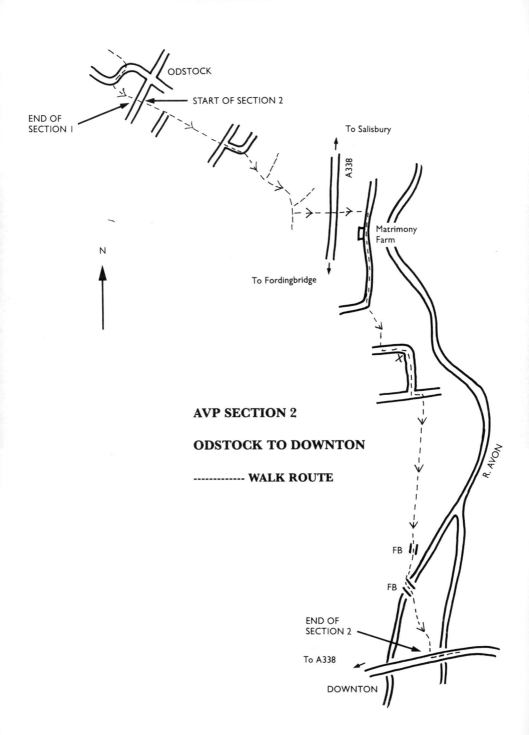

ODSTOCK

START OF SECTION 2

END OF
SECTION I

To Salisbury

A338

Matrimony
Farm

To Fordingbridge

N

AVP SECTION 2

ODSTOCK TO DOWNTON

------------- **WALK ROUTE**

R. AVON

FB

FB

END OF
SECTION 2

To A338

DOWNTON

Wood Green Common.

When the road bears right out of the village, turn left at a gravel road leading to several houses. After 50 yards, go right over a stile and head across the open fields on a clearly defined footpath to reach a stile onto a farm road. Turn left along this road, with a tributary of the Avon on the left. At the entrance to New Court Farm, turn left over a bridge (constructed of wood and metal) onto a gravel track. After 100 yards, where the track veers left at a wooden railway sleeper bridge, go straight ahead to follow a grass path. This soon joins the banks of the Avon and is a pleasant stroll over a footbridge and along a cinder path into Downton High Street.

To continue the walk, turn left here and follow the next set of instructions.

Those finishing the walk here can turn right and walk through the village to reach the A338 and the bus route (service X3).

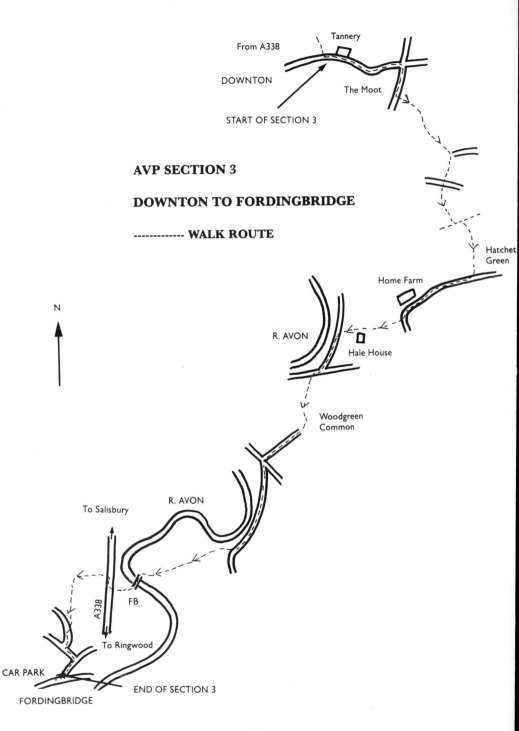

Tannery

From A338

DOWNTON

START OF SECTION 3

The Moot

AVP SECTION 3

DOWNTON TO FORDINGBRIDGE

------------ **WALK ROUTE**

Hatchet Green

Home Farm

N

R. AVON

Hale House

Woodgreen Common

To Salisbury

R. AVON

A338

FB

To Ringwood

CAR PARK

END OF SECTION 3

FORDINGBRIDGE

SECTION 3 — DOWNTON TO FORDINGBRIDGE — 7 miles
Contributed by Ernest Paine

Walkers starting this section at Downton and arriving there by bus (service X3) should alight at 'The Bull', turn into the B3080, Downton to Redlynch road, and walk almost half a mile to reach the bridge over the canal (GR 176214).

Motorists can usually park somewhere along this road and walk to the bridge.

Those who are already on the AVP and continuing through, will have followed the canal to emerge at the bridge and turn left.

This section of the path links two market towns both dating from early medieval times — Downton in Wiltshire and Fordingbridge in Hampshire — each with fascinating historical interest.

The path leaves the Avon at Downton in favour of the higher ground to the east, following downs, fields and woods until it descends from the Iron Age Castle Hill Fort to the flood plain, one and a half miles from Fordingbridge.

The Route

From the bridge, continue along the High Street (east) to pass a large building — the Tannery — on the left. Just beyond 'The Wooden Spoon' public house, turn right into Moot Lane and soon observe on the right (and visit if time) the famous Downton Moot, where, in the past, villagers assembled to conduct publicly their form of local government. A little further on, a footpath sign directs left to Woodfalls Road, a lane climbing gently south-east to a stile. Follow in the same direction beneath power lines for almost half a mile. Cross a stile on the right and continue uphill (south-south-east) to a farm track. Turn right (but pause to look back and admire the view) and go over a cross track via two stiles. Continue down the field, over a stile and uphill to two more stiles. A track (south-south-east) leads into a field. Find another stile in the hedge near a prominent signpost and follow the direction of a second post diagonally across the field, below wires, to reach a stile beneath trees. Beyond, follow the right-hand edge of the field downhill, over a green-painted gate and a stream with a plank bridge.

The route now rises through woodland to a stile into a field. Continue in the same direction, on the right of a fenced inclosure, and cross a stile to a cottage on the right. A gravel track leads to a minor road at Hatchet Green (GR192192). The last mile can be muddy after rain.

From Hatchet Green, turn right into a minor road (west-south-west) for half a mile and, after a left-hand bend, find a footpath sign on the right shortly before an avenue of trees. These lead down to the imposing Georgian mansion — Hale House — built in 1715. The gravelled footpath runs parallel to and on the right of the drive, then passes St. Mary's Church to reach a minor road close to the river Avon again.

Turn left (south) along the road with trees on the right obscuring views of the river. In about a quarter of a mile, at a triangular junction, turn right, but in a few yards enter the drive to Hale Rectory on the left and cross a small stile between a cattle-grid and a five-barred gate. A grassy path follows alongside the hedge through three meadows divided by gates and stiles and emerges onto a gravel track. Continue straight ahead, climbing steadily, then bear left with village houses on each side. At the top, bear right along the Woodgreen road, cross over and continue south across the right-hand side of the Common. Bear slightly right down a lane which winds to meet a road. Here turn left on the AVP. (Anyone wishing to end the walk here could continue on the road, westwards, through Woodgreen to reach the bus route on the A338 at Breamore.)

Opposite the 'Cemetery' signpost, turn right on the Castle Hill Road and enjoy fine views of the river and valley below for about three-quarters of a mile.

At the bottom of the hill, immediately after passing a house on the right named 'Armsley', turn right and go down to a gate with a prominent AVP signpost. This leads to a travel track. Ignore a footpath on the left and continue (west-south-west) for nearly half a mile, across water meadows with drainage streams and concrete bridges, to a suspension footbridge which gives access through Burgate Manor Farm to the busy A338.

(There are bus stops on each side of the road here for those who have walked far enough.)

Cross the road and turn right, passing the 14th century 'Tudor Rose'. Soon, at a footpath sign, turn left and find another signpost directing east between a farm and a cart track. After about 400 yards, turn left and the route into Fordingbridge passes a school on the left, emerges into an estate, then turns right along Penny's Lane. Where the road joins Green Lane, follow signs ahead to the car park.

To continue on the AVP, follow the next set of instructions.

Those finishing their walk here, and without a car, can catch a bus (service X3) from the Town Centre back to Downton or on to Salisbury.

SECTION 4 — FORDINGBRIDGE TO IBSLEY — 4 miles
Contributed by Anne and Trevor Davies

Fordingbridge has a very large, free Central Car Park (GR 148143) and another, smaller parking area on the slip road from the A338 into town.

It can be reached by bus (service X3) from Salisbury or from Poole/Bournemouth/Ringwood. The bus stops at Fordingbridge Post Office, near the Central Car Park.

After leaving Fordingbridge, the path soon enters watermeadows which may be somewhat waterlogged if there has been heavy rain. However, during this section the walker will know that the Avon is never far away. It is possible to divert slightly in order to visit the trout farm at Bicton Mill. Those who do not know this area will be surprised to see the unspoiled village of Harbridge Green and Turmer, recently reprieved from the threat of further gravel extraction.

The Route

Leave the car park by the eastern entrance, near the toilet block, and turn right to join the High Street by the National Westminster Bank. Continue along the High Street for about 200 yards to a road junction and take the left-hand fork (the Alderholt road). Where the road curves left, pass an interesting terrace of almshouses dated 1919, then on to St. Mary's Church where the path goes through the churchyard. It is well worth visiting the church before proceeding. From the main church gate, bear left, round the eastern end of the church and in about 50 yards there is an AVP sign pointing south.

Continue along this fenced path for about 800 yards passing a water treatment plant on the right. Go over another stile then cross a field, veering left (south-east). In the corner, cross a stile, then a small concrete bridge. After a further 50 yards, look for a stile under some trees on the right.

(Those who wish may, before crossing this stile, continue south-east for about 400 yards to visit Bicton Mill Trout Farm on the opposite bank of the river.)

Having crossed the stile under the trees, proceed in a southerly direction with the river on the left. After about 500 yards cross two stiles in rapid succession (with an animal pound on the left between them) to reach a tree-lined cart track. Turn right (west) along this for about 150 yards to reach two stiles close together on the left.

Having scaled these, continue just east of south across damp meadowland for about 500 yards to reach a stile into another field. Turn right (south-west), keeping to the field edge to reach a fenced

15

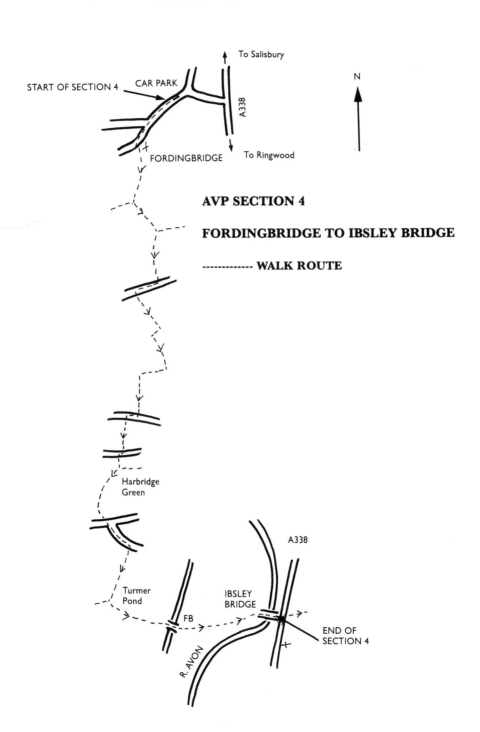

START OF SECTION 4

CAR PARK

To Salisbury

A338

FORDINGBRIDGE

To Ringwood

N

AVP SECTION 4

FORDINGBRIDGE TO IBSLEY BRIDGE

------------- **WALK ROUTE**

Harbridge
Green

A338

Turmer
Pond

IBSLEY
BRIDGE

FB

END OF
SECTION 4

R. AVON

The bridge over the Avon at Fordingbridge is believed to date from Norman times.

Below: The Ibsley bridge.

water channel. Turn left and follow this in a southerly direction. About 300 yards on, cross a stile and a wooden footbridge over the channel.

Here the AVP climbs away from the river for a while. Follow the fence between two fields in a westerly direction for about 400 yards, then turn left (south) onto a farm track which leads to North End Farm. Turn right (west) onto the metalled road for about 100 yards to a stile on the left. Cross two fields, going south. A stile under one of the mature oak trees leads onto a fenced path for 100 yards alongside private gardens. Cross a stile onto a metalled road through the delightful village of Harbridge Green. Turn right (west) on the road for 50 yards, then left (south) opposite a thatched cottage.

Follow this hardcore track for about 400 yards, passing an interesting thatched house on the left. At Cobley Cottage, the end of the track, veer right through a gateway into a field. Turn left (south-west) and cross the field to exit onto a metalled road. Go left (south-east) along the road for about 300 yards to a stile in the hedge on the right. Cross one field (south) and pass along the edge of a second (copse on the right and views of Harbridge Church on the left). Cross a stile into a larger field and continue with the fence still on the right. About 200 yards across the field, Harbridge Farm on the right has an interesting collection of old farm machinery on view in the yard. Cross a stile in the fence on the right and in 20 yards the path emerges onto the gravel roads around Turmer village green and pond.

Turn left (south-east) along the gravel road for about 400 yards. When the road turns sharply left, carry straight on through a kissing gate and across a stream. A stile leads into a field which the path crosses (east) to reach the north bank of the Avon. Follow the river bank (easterly) and cross two stiles. Turning slightly left, the path leaves the river bank, passes between gnarled willow trees and heads for the attractive Ibsley Bridge about 200 yards away where the river Avon flows peacefully alongside the busy A338. The AVP continues through the farm immediately opposite.

This road is on the bus route (service X3) for those who wish to finish here.

SECTION 5 — IBSLEY BRIDGE TO RINGWOOD — 5 miles
Contributed by Vic Ruston

It is possible to park cars on the roadside west of Ibsley Bridge (GR 150097). Buses (service X3) from Salisbury in the north or Poole/Bournemouth/Ringwood to the south, stop at Ibsley Church, about 400 yard south of the bridge.

The AVP now crosses several different types of terrain, including farmland, and rises gently to enter the perambulation of the New Forest. There are lovely views across the valley before reaching the lakes where birds abound.

The Route
From Ibsley Bridge, cross the A338 to a footpath leading into a farmyard directly opposite. Walk between the fence and the hedge, over the stile and across two fields, keeping the hedge on the left. Cross the stile in the corner of the field and turn left (north). Keep to the edge of the field with the fence and hedge on the right. Cross the double stile and continue in the same direction until the path swings through the hedge and over a stile. Now go diagonally across the field, between crops, in an easterly direction. Head for a point about 20 yards to the left of a house, cross three stiles in succession and proceed in the same direction across two fields, keeping the hedge and buildings on the right. A stile leads onto a minor road. Cross the road, bearing right to reach the entrance drive to the village hall. The path is to the right of the cattle grid.

Keep the hedge on the left until crossing a stile where a well-defined path leads uphill across two fields (east). Cross the stile at the top of the fields leading to the garden wall of a house and turn right (south). The track swings slowly to the left and contours around Summerlug Hill. In about 100 yards it drops to the right onto a gravel road. Go straight across the road, over a ditch (sleeper bridge), up the rise and, at the top, swing right (south) with a fence on the right and bracken-covered hillside on the left. (Along this stretch are views across the lakes and the remains of the wartime airfield with Somerley House in the background to the left.)

Approaching Newlands Plantation, look for a stile in the fence to the right of the wood. Cross two fields (south) and over stiles to the minor road. Turn left along the road and pass Moyles Court (now a school but once the home of Dame Alicia Lisle who was sentenced to death by Judge Jefferies).

Cross the ford (Dockens Water) and turn right to follow the stream. On reaching Ellingham Road look for and cross a stile about 20 yards

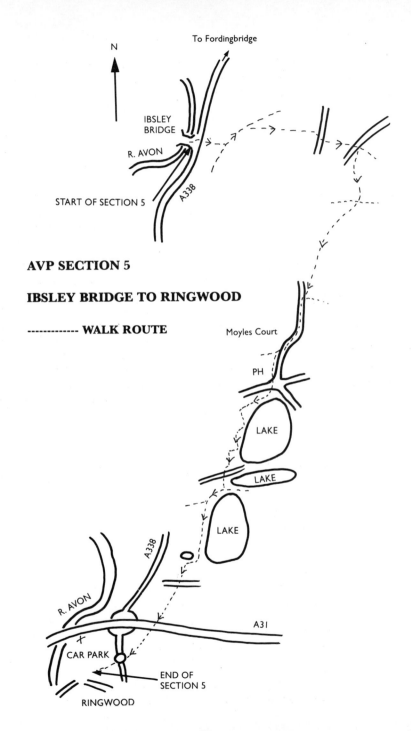

To Fordingbridge

N

IBSLEY
BRIDGE

R. AVON

A338

START OF SECTION 5

AVP SECTION 5

IBSLEY BRIDGE TO RINGWOOD

------------ **WALK ROUTE**

Moyles Court

PH

LAKE

LAKE

LAKE

A338

R. AVON

A31

CAR PARK

END OF
SECTION 5

RINGWOOD

20

along this road, on the left. The path is parallel to the road until it reaches the 'Alice Lisle' public house. Here continue along the road, over the cattle grid, past a telephone box to a small gate beside Ivy Cottage. Go through the gate and swing right (west), past the cottages and with a lake on the left. Turn right at the first of the Sailing Club gates and follow the grass track between hedges. On the far side of the second of the Sailing Club gates take the path going left (south) through the staggered fence. The path swings west then south again between two lakes and crosses a metal stile onto a gravel road. Turn right and in 50 yards take the path on the left over a stile with a lake on the left and a garden on the right. The path swings right passing a group of trees planted by local Councillors to commemorate the Queen's 40th anniversary.

Look for a small footbridge on the left and cross the stream here. From the end of the bridge bear right and cross a field entrance through staggered stiles. Continue south through trees with the stream now on the right. On reaching a housing estate, turn right and follow the pavement on the right. Before the end of the estate, cross the road into Linbrook Court, which soon becomes a gravel path. Cross Northfield Road into Gravel Lane. Look carefully for traffic at the underpass then proceed straight ahead until, just before the traffic roundabout, turn right and cross the dual carriageway. At the other side, turn left and cross the road into a footpath that runs between two sections of the car park. Signs point ahead to the Information Centre and toilets and the next section of the AVP continues from there.

Bus stops (service X3 and others) are on the south side of the car park.

THE COUNTRYSIDE CODE
Guard against all risk of fire.
Fasten all gates.
Keep dogs under proper control.
Keep to paths across farmland.
Avoid damaging fences, hedges and walls.
Leave no litter — take it home.
Safeguard all water supplies.
Protect wildlife, wild plants and trees.
Go carefully on country roads.
Respect the life of the countryside.

Take nothing but photographs
Leave nothing but footprints.

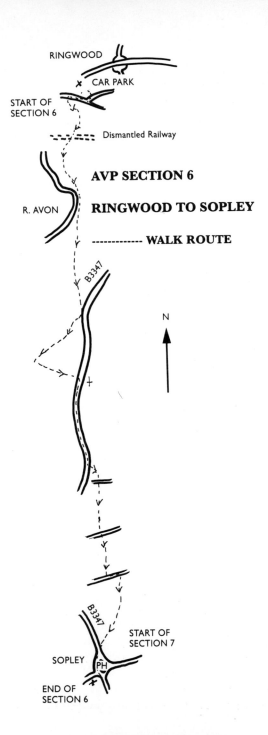

RINGWOOD

CAR PARK

START OF
SECTION 6

- - - - Dismantled Railway

AVP SECTION 6

RINGWOOD TO SOPLEY

R. AVON

------------ **WALK ROUTE**

B3347

N

B3347

SOPLEY

PH

START OF
SECTION 7

END OF
SECTION 6

SECTION 6 — RINGWOOD TO SOPLEY — 6.5 miles
Contributed by Jim and Marjorie Kerr

Those who have arrived by car should follow the signs for the Information Centre (GR 157054) whilst those reaching Ringwood by bus will have dismounted just past this building. There is a variety of bus services to Ringwood from all directions (check locally).

Anyone coming through from Ibsley will have reached Ringwood at a small roundabout adjacent to the Car Park where there is a fingerpost pointing through the cars towards the toilets and the Information Centre.

Here the walk soon leaves the town and crosses delightful water meadows which may be flooded after heavy rain. Unfortunately there is a section alongside a busy road at Bisterne and attempts to obtain a field-path were unsuccessful. However, given good weather, this is a pleasant walk leading to an interesting old hamlet.

The Route

Opposite the Information Centre is a narrow road — Meeting House Lane — which leads towards the Market Place.

At the Market Place turn right, pass the White Hart and where the road divides at a central area used for auctions on Market Day (Wednesday), take the left fork — West Street. Go past a few shops and several houses and the attractive thatched 'Old Cottage Restaurant'.

Continue along the road which crosses the river, then turn left beside a building marked 'Ringwood Tackle'. The gravel drive leads through a small caravan park and in about 100 yards cross a waymarked stile leading into a field.

Bear half left and follow the path towards a bridge with metal railings. Turn left to cross this bridge and follow a small track towards houses.

Bear right on a little gravel track in front of Bickerley Cottages. At the end of the houses turn right and immediately after a house called 'Riverside', where the track divides, take the right-hand fork leading south.

After passing a few cottages on the left, recross the river by a bridge. Continue straight ahead over the disused railway track by a gate and a stile. Within a few yards bear right, away from the main path. This section is likely to be very wet but there are a few plank bridges leading to a stile. Cross this and turn left alongside the field boundary. Where the fence ends on the left, continue straight ahead in the same direction through fields.

Within 200 or 300 yards turn left at a post and walk towards the end of a line of straggly trees. A plank helps cross a very wet section.

Continue in the direction of the plank, still across fields, towards a white notice board ahead by a gap.

Now regain the river on the right-hand side. After about 50 yards, head half left, away from the river, towards a stile on which there is a large yellow marker. The path rejoins the river in about another 150 to 200 yards. There are three bridges to cross, then turn left onto a fairly wide junction of tracks. Turn right at this junction and continue along a shingle track. When this is joined by another path on the left, bear slightly right, generally in a southerly direction. Ignore footpath signs leading off the track. Soon reach open grassland on both sides then two or three houses on the left.

In about 200 yards after the cottages, the path goes straight ahead onto a grassy track where a fingerpost points in the correct direction.

Within a short distance this path veers slightly left to cross a stile. Go ahead, ignoring a track on the right, to reach a stile on the left. Cross this and follow the direction of the AVP markers to reach another fingerpost, then over another stile and along the edge of a field.

In about 30 to 40 yards cross another stile on the left into a field. Drift away from the right-hand field boundary towards a stile and a fingerpost leading out onto the Ringwood to Christchurch road. Turn right, take the first turning on the right shortly before a telephone box then left onto a well-marked track. Pass cottages and a small building — Parkwood Engineering. When the shingle path turns sharply left, continue straight ahead on a grass track towards another fingerpost.

After another 70 to 80 yards turn right into a lane lined with magnificent oak trees. Pass a cottage on the right and immediately turn left by a fingerpost. Follow the field boundary on the left to reach the entrance to another field with a fingerpost pointing along the path, which is a narrow strip between two fields. This leads across a stile and into a gully, soon reaching the road via a gate.

Turn right opposite Bisterne Church and now walk along the grass verge by the busy road for about three-quarters of a mile. About 250 yards past Lower Bisterne Farm, on the left-hand side of the road can be seen the familiar AVP sign at a kissing gate, shortly before Tyrell's Ford Hotel. This is a newly negotiated right-of-way.

The path bends slightly right, and continues in a southerly direction, crossing straight over three farm lanes or tracks with good stiles or kissing gates. At the end of the third field, stiles lead through a small copse. There is then a wood on the right and an open field on the left. At the next exit onto a farm road, turn left along the road. Follow this for just over 100 yards and turn right through a kissing gate onto

Rhododendrons near Bisterne.

a path with a stream on the left. There are three stiles fairly close together before coming out into a field. The stream disappears into the trees but can still be heard gurgling.

Another stile is crossed, the stream reappears on the left and soon there are houses on the right. The path leads out onto the road just before the Sopley Forge and almost opposite Sopley Stores. There are several possibilities for B&B here.

Where the road divides take the right-hand fork to reach a road leading towards Sopley Mill (now a restaurant) and Sopley Church, both worth seeing. Either fork leads to the 'The Woolpack Inn'.

Those who have walked far enough may be able to catch a bus (service 105/ 115) from here to Ringwood or Christchurch – but NOT on Sundays or public holidays.

Sopley Church.

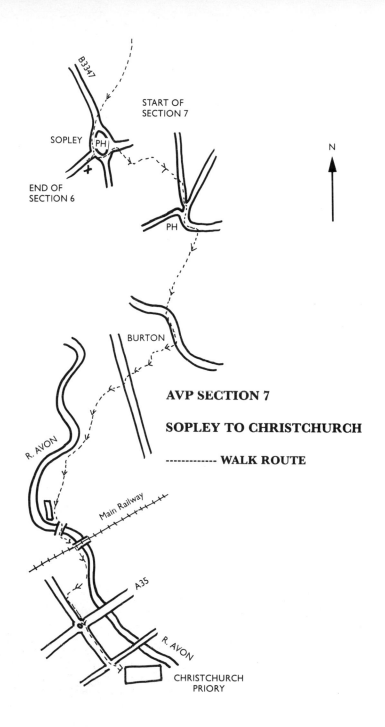

B3347

START OF
SECTION 7

SOPLEY
PH

END OF
SECTION 6

N

PH

BURTON

AVP SECTION 7

SOPLEY TO CHRISTCHURCH

------------ **WALK ROUTE**

R. AVON

Main Railway

A35

R. AVON

CHRISTCHURCH
PRIORY

Lane south of Ringwood on the Avon Valley Path.

Below: 'The Woolpack' at Sopley.

SECTION 7 — SOPLEY TO CHRISTCHURCH — 3.5 miles
Contributed by Jim and Marjorie Kerr

Having walked from Ringwood thus far, it is better to continue straight onto this section if possible. However, it may be possible to park a car in the lane leading to the church or ask permission to leave it in the car park of 'The Woolpack' (GR 157968).

The rather infrequent bus (service 105/115) between Christchurch and Ringwood goes through Sopley but does NOT run on Sundays or Bank Holidays.

It is worthwhile visiting both the church and the old mill (now a restaurant) before setting out from Sopley. On this last section of the walk we shall regain the banks of the Avon, but just beforehand part of the Burton housing estate will be encountered. Unfortunately the waymarks are often removed here so follow the directions carefully.

The Route

By the corner of 'The Woolpack' public house, cross the road towards a driveway between brick pillars, beside a house with a curved frontage. (Ignore a notice directing people to the main entrance to Morelands Christian College.) Beside the right-hand pillar is a very old well reputed to have supplied water for many cottages in the area. Go along this drive and within 100 yards enter a kissing gate on the left, walk parallel to the drive initially then turn left and over a stile into a field. Turn right and follow round the edge of the field. Just past a large house cross a stile on the right and bear slightly left across fields via three more stiles to a minor road.

At the road, turn right and continue to reach a busy road with The Lamb Inn opposite. Cross over and take a narrow road to the left of the inn. In about 30 to 40 yards the road crosses a stream and there is our path on the right (waymarked). Continue along this narrow path for about half a mile to reach the road near Burton Hall. Cross the road, turn left and walk along the pavement in front of this large building. Pass Burton Hall Close; after several houses there is a path leading right into the housing estate with a thatched house on the left.

A fingerpost points the way. At the end of the first group of houses (on the right), when a road is reached, turn left for about ten yards and then right into another grassy path behind houses. Immediately before the next road, a path bears off on the left. Continue along this with a thatched house on the left and in about 20 yards turn right through a gap in the railings. Cross the road and go ahead by another grassy area with children's swings on the right. Follow the tarmac path, cross the next road and continue ahead with another play area on the left. The track crosses a stream and continues down to the main road coming from the Christchurch bypass.

The wonderful Norman Christchurch Priory.

At the road turn left, passing a telephone box, and in about 20 yards cross the road and turn right by a fingerpost, cross two stiles and head for a small bridge over a wet area. Bear half left (due south) across the watermeadows with a trig point well over to the right.

It is important to head in the right direction as there are several plank-bridges to be crossed before the Avon River comes into view again. Here the river-side path is raised so turn left and follow this.

Shortly after crossing a stile, take a narrow path across the water meadows towards the Waterworks (head for a white bridge).

A waymarked kissing gate leads onto the causeway towards the pumping house. At this building, turn right and cross the bridge. Then, immediately turn left to find a narrow footpath between a temporary office building and the field boundary alongside the river. Presently we rejoin the Avon properly on the left. This now becomes a pleasant grassy walk. The path goes under a railway bridge, then behind houses to lead out into a cul-de-sac with several delightful cottages along it. Turn right and walk down to the main road into Christchurch.

Here turn left, walk along busy pavements towards a large roundabout. A pedestrian underpass leads to the High Street opposite. Go straight ahead, past the shops, to reach Christchurch Priory.

The bus back to Ringwood (service 105/115), via Sopley, stops outside the Old Town Hall which is half-way along the High Street on the left-hand side as you approach the Priory.

NB There is NO bus between Christchurch and Ringwood on Sundays and Bank Holidays.

This completes the Avon Valley Path walk.

WALKS in the HAMPSHIRE AVON VALLEY

Each of the following walks is designedto use part of the Avon Valley Path. Some of the walks can be used to provide an alternative route back after completing a section, so forming a circular walk.

ERICA and JOHN'S WALK — A SALISBURY CIRCULAR
8.5 miles or 11 miles

Salisbury is easily reached and the Cathedral, from whence the walk starts, is signposted. Refer to the notes given for the first section of the AVP as this walk starts on that route until just past Dogdean Farm.

The walk follows the Avon Valley Path from Salisbury to the valley of the River Ebble then turns into the lower Chalke Valley, passing through the typical Wiltshire village of Coombe Bissett to the attractive hamlet of Stratford Tony from where an extension is possible onto the downs, giving a sweeping view. In spring and summer the verges are bright with the wild flowers of the chalk downland.

From Stratford Tony it takes the line of the Roman road which ran from Badbury Rings to Old Sarum, then joins the Shaftesbury Drove or Herepath, an ancient route along the top of the downs from Salisbury to Shaftesbury. After the Salisbury Race-course, it cuts across towards Harnham with the Cathedral spire beckoning the walker back to the city.

The Route
Follow the directions for the Avon Valley path from Salisbury to beyond Dogdean Farm where the farm track goes down towards the River Ebble and reaches a wide grassy cross-track (GR 136266).

Ramblers on the Avon Valley Path.

Overleaf: The River Avon from Castle Hill.

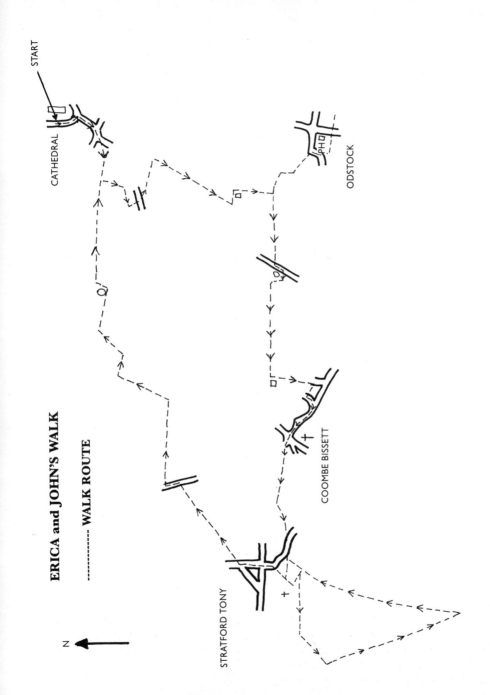

ERICA and JOHN'S WALK

------ WALK ROUTE

N

START

CATHEDRAL

ODSTOCK

COOMBE BISSETT

STRATFORD TONY

34

Turn right (west) along the grassy track for over half a mile until the Salisbury to Homington road is reached. Turn left (south-west) along the road for about 200 yards, passing the entrance to a house and crossing a small bridge. Immediately cross a stile on the right to go west then north. Pass an ornamental pond, cross a wooden bridge and go through a gate. Turn left (west) following the line of the stream. Cross a stile into the next field, then slightly right, slope upwards along the hillside keeping in a westerly direction to the next stile. Continue ahead on a contouring path towards a house.

At the house turn left (south) downhill — signposted 'Stockbridge Lane' — with old watercress beds to the right. In the valley, cross a footbridge, go through a gate to another bridge, then cross the field in the same direction to a kissing gate and a bridge which crosses the river. The path then comes out at the edge of Coombe Bissett into the start of a lane with cottages on the left.

About 100 yards beyond these look for a narrow path on the right (west) going up steps between boundaries. This leads into another lane. Go left uphill to reach the road. Here turn right and follow the road into the centre of the village, passing a shop, the church and green at the junction with the A354. (The pub is along the main road on the right.)

Cross the main road then go left for a few yards to reach the start of two tracks on the right-hand side of the road. Take the first (lower) track, signposted 'Stratford Tony', by the river (west). Go through a gate to Cranborne Cottage, cross a stile into a field and through a gate into the next field. Follow the fence round, ignoring a gate to a bridge. Cross the stile in the corner of the field and continue ahead through the next field (ignore a track to the river). At the end of the field go through a gate onto the road and turn right (west) past a bungalow into Stratford Tony. Keep to the south of the river and between it and cottages to reach a footbridge beyond the cottages.

Those who wish to keep to the shorter walk and do NOT want to add the extension should now miss the next paragraph and go to ＊.

Do not cross the footbridge but go half-left towards the small church. Just before it, turn left and in 20 yards, sharp right (west) along a footpath above the church. Continue between hedges for a quarter of a mile to Throope Manor. Pass between a long shed and cottages and follow the lane to the left at the end of the shed. Pass the Manor House on the right, go through gates, then straight ahead, uphill, on a concrete track. (Ignore the first track to the left.) After the last building, take the track to the left (south-east) which climbs up onto

The downs above Stratford Tony.

the downs, initially between trees and shrubs, for a mile. As it levels out there are expansive views along the Chalke Valley. Just before reaching a shrubby area, the track crosses a cattle grid.

Turn sharp left to pick up a different track back to Stratford Tony (north). In a mile the track drops down to the river. Turn left to reach the footbridge.

*Cross the footbridge and follow the path right to the road. Go left (north) to reach the crossroads with the main road along the Chalke Valley. Take the road ahead (north) to a junction 200 yards ahead. Here take the track on the right (north-east) — the Roman road. Once past a hay barn the track becomes overgrown then joins a stony cart-track. Follow this up the side of the field. Go through a gate and keeping north-east take the grassy track ahead to reach a road. Turn left (north-west) onto the road for 200 yards through trees to the Shaftesbury Drove. Turn right (east) along the Drove with the race course on the left. Shortly after the end of the course railings, and just before the power lines, turn left off the Drove.

The path should go through a thick hedge ahead and slightly to the right, but it is impassable. Therefore go down the headland to the right of it (north-east). Shortly after going under the power lines, the path ends at a gate which leads onto a cart track. A few yards on, leave the field at a barbed wire gate onto the track. Follow this in the same direction for a quarter of a mile until shortly after it starts to go downhill and turns left. Here turn right (east) into the second of two adjacent field entrances, keeping the fence on the right. At the end of this field follow the fence left (north) and in 100 yards go right (east) into another field.

Continue east towards a radio mast and group of trees. The path soon skirts the top of Harnham chalk pit with views across the City to the Cathedral. It becomes increasingly well-worn as it runs above the wooded slope and joins the Avon Valley Path at Bishop's Walk which leads east to Old Blandford Road.

Go down this road and then left along New Harnham Road to the playing field (just after St. Mary's Close). Cross the field to the river (a branch of the Nadder) for the 'Constable' view of the Cathedral across the water meadows. Follow the river upstream (north-east) to the medieval Old Harnham Mill. Take the path in front of the mill and continue north-west across the water meadows to the Elizabeth Gardens. Turn right into the centre of Salisbury.

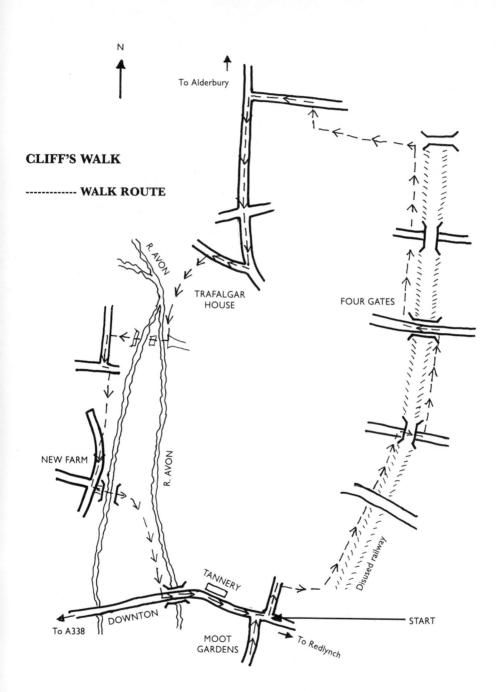

N

CLIFF'S WALK

------------- WALK ROUTE

To Alderbury

R. AVON

TRAFALGAR
HOUSE

FOUR GATES

R. AVON

NEW FARM

Disused railway

TANNERY

START

DOWNTON

To A338

MOOT
GARDENS

To Redlynch

Cottages at Downton.

CLIFF'S WALK — A DOWNTON CIRCULAR — 8 miles

The route can be reached by bus to 'The Bull' public house at Downton. Then walk about three-quarters of a mile along the High Street through the village to reach Barford Lane, the turning after 'The Wooden Spoon' (GR 182215).

If arriving by car, there is usually parking space in the Moot Garden Car Park, 200 yards along Moot Lane which is the right-hand turning off the High Street, just past 'The Wooden Spoon'. From the car park, return to the High Street and cross over to Barford Lane.

This circular walk follows part of the old Salisbury to Ringwood railway line, crosses the River Avon and joins the AVP in Charlton All Saints. A short detour from the main route allows a glimpse of historic Trafalgar House, gifted to Lord Nelson by a grateful nation.

While in Downton do visit the Moot Gardens which were laid out in the 18th century on the earthworks of a Norman Castle. They are in Moot Lane (see car parking advice).

The Route

Walk along Barford Lane for about 100 yards then turn right into a narrow, part-paved lane next to Wellesley Cottage and continue on a footpath leading to Hamilton Park. Cross the road to a continuation of the path, go over three stiles and follow the old railway line on the right to reach open farmland. Continue north-east and uphill across open fields, following a narrow, poorly-defined path and crossing a farm road. At the brow of the slope the continuing line of the old railway track can be seen straight ahead. Continue, downhill now, to join the footpath to the left of this.

After 50 yards, an old five-barred crossing gate allows access to the disused track. It is overgrown in places but passable for about three-quarters of a mile although the official path continues with the railway on the right. (If taking the railway track, after 15 to 20 minutes leave it on the right at a second set of old crossing gates before the track becomes too overgrown to continue. Rejoin the bridleway shortly before the second country road referred to below.)

Following the official path, soon reach a metalled country road. Turn right under the railway bridge and continue on a bridleway with the railway now on the left. Follow the line (north) to a second country road, turn left over a railway bridge and continue past 'Fourgates' cottage on the left with the railway again on the right. Pass through a six-barred metal gate and shortly thereafter a four-barred dilapidated wooden gate. Continue, still with the railway on the right, across a metalled farm road and up a gentle slope to a T-junction.

Here leave the railway and turn left along a well-defined path towards a small wood. Follow the footpath into the woods, bear right immediately and continue on the path, now bearing left along the edge of the wood. After 180 yards, where the path divides, bear right, out of the woods, and walk north with the wood now on the right. Pass under a power line, turn left at a dirt road and walk out to the Alderbury road.

Turn left and follow the tarmac for just under one mile passing Witherington Farm on the right. As the road sweeps downhill, watch for a concrete road on the right with an attractive view below of the Avon and Charlton All Saints. Take this road and after 200 yards turn left into the woods (bridleway sign). Now bear right (south-west) following an indistinct, overgrown path signed by fading yellow bands on trees. After descending a steep slope, in 60 to 70 yards the path and signs become clearer.

Shortly thereafter the Avon comes into view with houses beyond the fields. Continue above the river bank and soon join a wider path coming in from the left. When the path leads to a concrete track, turn right and walk down to the weir house or, if you wish to view Trafalgar House, turn left. Continue on the track for about 200 yards and shortly after passing a cottage on the right the house can be seen across the open grounds. Retrace your steps to rejoin the walk.

At the weir house, bear right to cross several footbridges over the Avon. Follow the footpath through a single five-barred gate, over two further footbridges and through an old-fashioned metal turnstile into Charlton All Saints. Turn left into the main street to join the Avon Valley Path and follow the walk directions from the village to Downton as set out in the Odstock to Downton section of this book.

Saxon Church, Breamore.

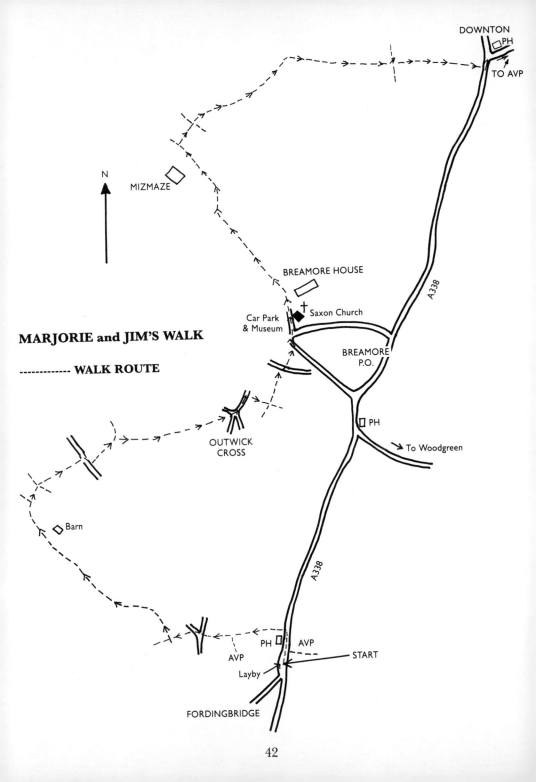

DOWNTON

PH

TO AVP

N

MIZMAZE

A338

BREAMORE HOUSE

Car Park & Museum

† Saxon Church

BREAMORE P.O.

MARJORIE and JIM'S WALK

------------ **WALK ROUTE**

PH

To Woodgreen

OUTWICK CROSS

Barn

A338

PH

AVP

START

AVP

Layby

FORDINGBRIDGE

42

MARJORIE and JIM'S WALK — FORDINGBRIDGE — BREAMORE — DOWNTON — 6 or 9 miles (linear walks); 10 or 16 miles (circular walks)

This walk starts from Lower Burgate, on the A338 north of Fordingbridge where the Avon Valley path crosses the road. There are bus stops close to this point. Cars may be parked in a layby just south of 'The Hour Glass' restaurant — near the entrance to Burgate School — reached from the road leading into Fordingbridge (GR 152155). If preferring to use the main Fordingbridge Car Park, go northwards from there on the Whitsbury road and follow the AVP signs until reaching the cross track from Lower Burgate then turn left.

Those choosing the shorter linear distance can walk down to the A338 at Breamore to catch a bus back, while for the ten-mile circular, walkers who do not mind some road-walking, could, from the A338, follow the minor road to Woodgreen (south of 'The Bat and Ball') and join the AVP there. The nine-mile linear walk finishes at Downton. Walking back from here to Fordingbridge would make a circular walk of nearly 16 miles.

This walk follows a stream which is a tributary of the Avon, turns north through woodland, then crosses fields to reach Breamore Park where some walkers may wish to visit Breamore House, Museums and Church. These are open most days of the week during the summer, but only on selected days during the rest of the year. Check with the Tourist Information Office.

The Route

From the layby turn towards Salisbury on the west side of the A338, and just past 'The Tudor Rose', turn left onto the waymarked AVP route. In about 300 yards ignore the AVP turning on the left (or join the walk here if parking in Fordingbridge) and continue ahead (west) to reach a minor road. Turn left and, almost immediately, right into Whitsbury Road. Soon take a lane on the left (south-west) and in about 200 yards, just past an electricity sub-station, look for a narrow footpath through the trees on the right. Follow this, turning left into the trees, and after about 100 yards cross a stile into a field.

The path continues straight ahead (north-west) with the hedge on the right at first. At a cross track turn left for a few paces, then right, still generally north-west, into a little wood. Where the wood ends, turn left and follow the edge of the field with trees on the left. In about 200 yards look carefully for a stile on the left leading into the trees. The path continues north-west with Sweatford Water on the left and a boundary on the right. (In the summer the stream will probably be dry.)

Two more stiles lead out into fields again and, keeping the hedge on the left, continue through three fields still in the same direction. (Clack Barn will be visible in the top right-hand corner of the third field.) The path hugs the edge of the wood then leads through a corner of woodland, turning right, then bearing left, and emerging to join a track coming down from the barn. This turns slightly left to a gate and stile. Cross the stile and the path now veers slightly right with the field boundary first on the right and then the left. Cross another stile beside a gate and at a path junction turn right (almost due north).

Soon a cross track is met, but go straight over this and look for an indistinct path immediately ahead rising very steeply (north-east) — a handrail has been promised here. This leads to a stile and into a field. Turn left, with woods on the left at first, to reach a gate. Cross the field and go through another gate onto a cross track. Turn right and in about 20 yards there is a footpath signposted on the left. This leads slightly downhill through woods with, presently, a steep drop on the right. At a junction of paths by a tall oak tree, take the left path down a little bank (the other one leads to a private driveway). After passing alongside a garden the path reaches the minor road from Fordingbridge to Whitsbury. At the road turn right and within a few paces turn left into Radnall Wood (north-east). This a bridleway and can be muddy in places.

Keep to the main track but after about 500 yards, when the track turns left, take a faint path on the right (south-east) — there is a yellow circle on an oak tree. Continue along this path for about 50 yards to reach a wide cross track. Yellow waymarks then indicate a path, slightly left, through the woods. Follow this and on emerging from the woods cross the stile immediately opposite and continue through the field (east) towards a stile ahead. This leads into another woodland of tall trees and on emerging from them, go forward into a lane (north of east) and after crossing a stile and passing a cottage reach a crossroads (Outwick Cross).

Take the road ahead, waymarked 'Breamore', but after about 200 yards, immediately after two cottages, cross a stile on the right and follow the path across the field (south-east). Cross the next stile and turn left to follow the field edge (slightly east of north) and go through a gate to reach a lane. Turn right and in a few paces take a footpath on the left. The path bears left, then right to cross the middle of the field and goes down a steep bank to another lane. Turn left here to reach Breamore House, Museums and Church. The House and the Tea Barn will be open on most days during the summer months (check first).

To finish here turn right at this lane and walk down to the A338. Buses stop by the post office.

Wood Green Common.

Below: Ramblers on the bridge over the Avon at Hale.

Those wishing to walk back to Fordingbridge by the shortest route (ten miles) must also walk down to the A338, turn right first, then left after 'The Bat and Ball', crossing the Avon and passing the old mill. Woodgreen is about half a mile after the bridge. There turn right and follow the road for another half a mile onto Castle Hill to join the AVP and follow this back to Lower Burgate.

To continue to Downton for the nine-mile linear or 16 miles circular, follow signs for Breamore House, walk up the driveway past the House then uphill through the woods (famed for bluebells in Spring). After almost a mile, a cross track is reached (South Charnford Drove). Turn left (north-west) along the Drove and note that after about 150 yards, where the track bears right, there is a path on the left leading uphill to a clump of trees where the Miz Maze can be visited. After seeing this ancient monument, return to the Drove and continue along it for about a further 300 yards. At a junction of paths, turn right (east of north) on a short path with a wood on the left and a field on the right. There are good views across on the right to the eastern side of the Avon Valley.

On reaching a cross track (North Charnford Drove) turn left and almost immediately go through a little gate on the right into a field. Bear slightly right, diagonally downhill to a gap in the corner, then ahead, uphill to the next hedge (north-east) and through another little gate. Turn left and follow uphill, with the hedge on the left, to a cross track. Go through the hedge opposite and follow round the field, first right, then left, to exit onto a track from Botley's Farm (buildings can be seen on the left). Turn right here. The path may be very overgrown at first, but after about half a mile, becomes clearer.

After the track bears left, downhill to a cross track, turn right then first left towards Downton. On reaching houses, continue straight ahead through a passageway between fences, passing a recreation ground, allotments and houses to reach the A338 just south of 'The Bull'. From here buses can be caught back to Lower Burford, Fordingbridge or Salisbury. Stalwarts who wish to walk back to Fordingbridge, should take the road almost opposite (marked 'Redlynch') and follow directions for the Downton to Fordingbridge section of the AVP.

ANNE and TREVOR'S WALK — IBSLEY BRIDGE TO FORDINGBRIDGE
4.5 miles (linear walk); 8.5 miles (circular walk)

Ibsley Bridge on the A338 (GR150097), can be reached by bus from Ringwood or Fordingbridge.

There is limited parking space by Ibsley Church or on the roadside just across the Bridge.

This is an easy walk east of the river, across farmland and across Gorley Common before rising to the hamlet of Hyde. On reaching Fordingbridge, walkers can follow the appropriate section of the Avon Valley Path to return to Ibsley, making a pleasant 8.5 mile round walk. Alternatively, the return can be made by bus.

The Route
From Ibsley Bridge, cross the A338 onto the Avon Valley Path route immediately opposite. Set off in an easterly direction for about 200 yards, turn left (north-east) onto another path along the field edge, then through some bushes to emerge after about 250 yards into a field. At this point, leave the AVP (which goes across the field due east).

Continue north-east to a stile in a hedge (there may be a diversion around the field edge during gravel extraction). Head north-east across a field to a stile right of a wooden building and, within a short distance, two more stiles. The path goes behind sheds to reach a stile leading into an unmetalled road. Cross this, go over a stile and, continuing north-east, yet another stile just right of a white house leads within about 100 yards to a high stile and reaches another unmetalled road. Almost opposite, cross another stile and the path runs diagonally through a field to yet another stile. Go on diagonally (still north-east) to a stile leading into a nursery garden. Bear half right and take a fenced path between houses for about 100 yards to a tarmacked drive and onto a road. At the road turn left to reach the triangular green of South Gorley about one mile from the start and with, possibly, a record density of stiles!

At the Green, take the right fork (marked 'Furze Hill') and after about 300 yards a stile on the left leads to a path across a field in a northerly direction. Cross the bridge over Huckles Brook and proceed uphill in the same direction along a fenced path for about 150 yards to emerge onto a wooded gravel track running east-west. Cross this, still going north, and skirt round the fenced wood passing a little gate marked Gorley Firs. Follow the fence around to reach a track going uphill (east-north-east) onto Gorley Common. The track turns north-north-east and crosses the top of the Common, a distance of about three-quarters of a mile. At the north-east part of the Common,

Above: Breamore House. Below: A stream near Turmer.

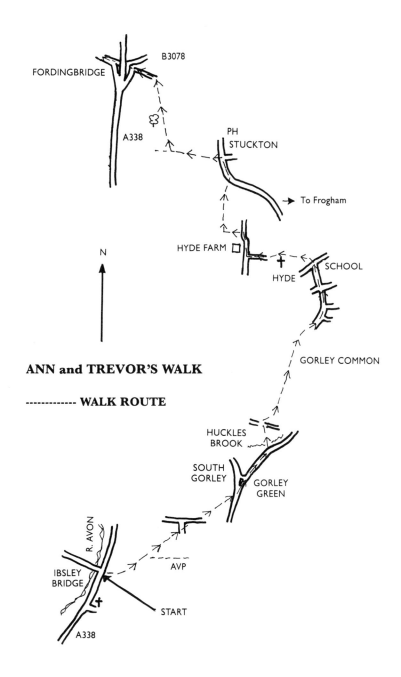

FORDINGBRIDGE

B3078

A338

PH
STUCKTON

→ To Frogham

N

HYDE FARM

HYDE

SCHOOL

ANN and TREVOR'S WALK

GORLEY COMMON

------------- **WALK ROUTE**

HUCKLES
BROOK

SOUTH
GORLEY

GORLEY
GREEN

R. AVON

AVP

IBSLEY
BRIDGE

START

A338

it reaches a road on the edge of Hyde. Turn and follow this road, passing a crossroads, for about 500 yards to Hyde School and a crossroads by the heath. Here, take the second left road (west) waymarked 'Hyde Church'. At the church turn right then left, following the boundary of the church grounds (west). Keep close to the hedge on the left then go down a steep bank to a tarmacked drive leading to a lane (Hyde Lane). Turn right and follow the lane (north) passing Hyde Farm. Soon after a bend in the lane, look for a footpath through a gate on the left. This leads along the field edge (hedge on the left) and after a second gate turn right (due north) and proceed along the edge of the field. A stile leads to a narrow path with a low garden wall on the right and then reaches a minor road (Frogham to Stuckton). Turn left and in about 250 yards look for a concealed path (signposted) on the left, just opposite a road turning. Take this path (west), following the edge of fields for about 500 yards, crossing two stiles, and just before a gateway turn right (north) immediately before the field-edge to a stile in the corner, with a small copse in the background.

Follow the path via several stiles and gates, passing the copse, heading north for about half a mile to reach a minor road. Here turn left (east) along the road for about 300 yards. Turn right to reach the B3078, then left, under the A338, and on into Fordingbridge.

VIC'S WALK

------- **WALK ROUTE**

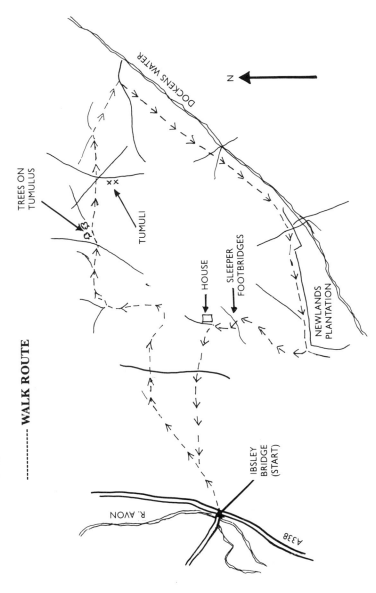

N

DOCKENS WATER

TREES ON
TUMULUS

TUMULI

HOUSE

SLEEPER
FOOTBRIDGES

NEWLANDS
PLANTATION

R. AVON

IBSLEY
BRIDGE
(START)

A338

VIC'S WALK — IBSLEY CIRCULAR — 6 miles

This circular walk starts from Ibsley Bridge (GR 150097), which is on the bus service from Ringwood to Salisbury.

Car parking is possible just over the bridge on the side of the road to Harbridge.

The walk begins on the Avon Valley Path but soon leaves it to enter the New Forest and go across the higher, open land of Ibsley Common. There are wide views from here. It returns alongside Dockens Water (a tributary of the Avon) and after skirting Summerlug Hill, finally rejoins the AVP.

The Route

From Ibsley Bridge, cross the A338 to the footpath directly opposite, beside the farmyard. Walk between the fence and hedge, cross the stile and then two fields, with the hedge on the left. Go over another stile in the corner of the field and turn left (north-east) along the edge of the field now with the fence and hedge on the right.

After a double stile, continue in the same direction until the path swings through the hedge and over a stile. Now leave the AVP and follow the hedge to the left. When the hedge turns left, keep close to it around the end of the field (a recent diversion). From the corner where the hedge turns right, in approximately 100 yards, look for a stile in the hedge. Cross this and go diagonally across the field heading for tall trees on the far side, to find another stile just to the right of these. Continue on the same line to yet another stile (in view) and after crossing this into a paddock, keep close to the hedge on the left. A stile is crossed into a gravelled lane. Cross this to another stile, then continue across the field to a stile in the far corner.

On reaching another gravelled road, turn right and walk eastwards to reach a cattle grid and a minor road. Turn left (north) along this for 50 yards, then right (east) to pass Newtown Farm. The road soon deteriorates into a track, and where it divides go part-left between houses for about 100 yards before turning left again to a stile on the left of a farm gate. Cross the stile and keep close to the deer fence on the right. The path leads northwards across the field to a wooden footbridge over a stream.

Continue straight ahead on a track up into the trees (still north). At the top of the rise the trees thin out and the track becomes grassy for a short stretch then meets a wide gravel track coming from the right. Turn right (east) and follow this track uphill, twisting but reaching the shoulder with a valley on both sides. The track climbs very slowly up to a small spinney of tall pine trees just to the left

Field paths at Ibsley.

of the track, standing on a small mound (a tumulus). The trees can be seen from a long way on the track giving a good point to aim for. There are wonderful views in all directions.

About 25 yards beyond the trees, the track divides. Take the path to the right (south-east) reaching a junction of several paths in about 500 yards. Take the one directly opposite and continue in the same direction, soon bearing slightly right to descend into the valley. On reaching a very sandy area where several paths meet, turn right (south-west) and follow the lower track along the valley bottom, ignoring the higher track back up the hill. Follow the contours just above the marshy area that runs down to Dockens Water where plenty of marsh flowers can be seen with huge swathes of bog asphodel in early July.

On reaching the wood take the track leading slightly right (west), heading for the high point about 200 yards away. This is Newlands Plantation — marked private. On reaching the corner, follow the track along the top side of the wood over a series of small hills and valleys. Before leaving this high ridge, look ahead at the views right across the Avon Valley.

Go down the hill and just before reaching the fence at the bottom, turn right (north) and join the AVP. Keep the fence on the left, even when it drops sharply on reaching a farm. Go over two sleeper bridges and up to a gravel track. Continue straight ahead across the track and up the bank on the far side for about 20 yards to where it swings left. Follow round the contour of the hill behind a row of houses. On reaching a large house on the right of the path, cross a stile in the hedge on the left and go downhill on a well-trodden path. Cross two fields and a small paddock to reach a cattle grid at the entrance to the village hall.

Cross the minor road and turn right but on the far side of the house almost opposite, take the stile in the corner of the field. Keeping the hedge on the left, cross two fields to reach Ibsley Manor Farm. Continue straight ahead (west) and go over three stiles very close together. Continue on the same line across another field to a stile in the far hedge and here rejoin the starting section of this walk. Cross the stile, turn left, keep the hedge on the left and cross the double stile, then walk on to the next stile. Turn right (west), with the hedge close on the right, go ahead to reach the A338 and Ibsley Bridge again.

DEREK'S WALK — A SOPLEY CIRCULAR — 6 miles or 4 miles

Sopley can be reached by bus from Ringwood or Christchurch but the service is not very frequent and does not run at all on Sundays.

Cars may be parked in the beginning of Sopley Lane or perhaps in the car park of 'The Woolpack' if you are returning there for refreshment, but do ask permission.

This is a typical area of level land in the Avon Valley, unspoiled by gravel extraction at the time of writing. There are wide, open views of the fields and plenty of game coverts to complement the picture.

The Route

The walk starts in Priest Lane, Sopley (GR 157971) and proceeds northwards along Priest Lane, soon becoming a grassy track into a field. Turn right along the boundary and left in the corner, following the high MoD fence on the right (underground are extensive remains of wartime RAF control rooms). Continue northwards past the end of this fence to meet a lane. Turn right here (east), go over a crossroads onto a farm track and past a pipeline station.

After a quarter of a mile there is a junction of five footpaths and bridleways, all waymarked. Take the second exit on the left (see map) and cross a stile. Cross three fields diagonally (north-east) and head for the left-hand end of a line of trees some way ahead. There are no stiles in the intervening hedges and fences but short lengths of rail near the line of the path. On reaching the trees, cross the brook by a bridge and continue easterly along a wooded path, with stiles, to open fields. The path follows the south side of a brook with a prominent embankment indicating a very old Forest boundary before the area was cleared for farming.

Half a mile from the bridge, at a stile, turn left through a small glade surrounded by trees, then in 100 yards cross the brook again by a bridge. The right of way now turns half-left to cut off the corner of the field and meets the fence on the left about 100 yards along.

Follow this fence northwards to reach a lane in a quarter of a mile. Here turn left along the lane for 200 yards, ignoring another lane junction from the right. A farm track will be found on the right leading to some large sheds at a timber yard. Just in front of the sheds the path turns left (west) through a pleasant wooded patch for nearly a mile to reach the road through Ripley. Here turn right along the road for the six-mile walk or go straight across for the shorter one.

Six-mile walk. Proceed northwards up the lane for a quarter of a mile and turn left at a footpath (signposted). Follow the path for

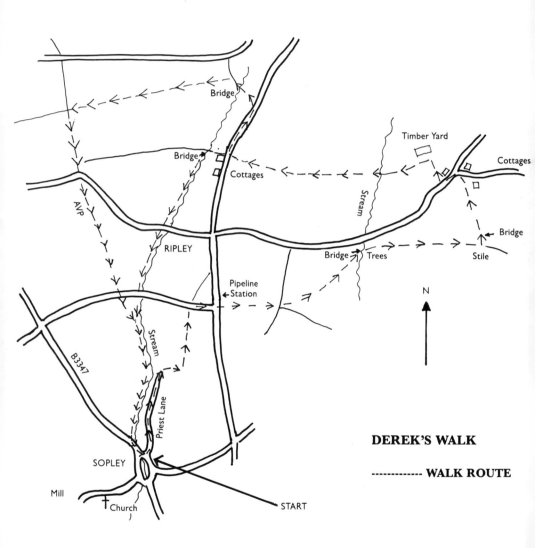

Bridge

Timber Yard

Cottages

Cottages

Bridge

Stream

Bridge

AVP

Stile

RIPLEY

Bridge   Trees

Pipeline
←Station

Stream

B3347

Priest Lane

DEREK'S WALK

SOPLEY

N

Mill

------------ **WALK ROUTE**

† Church

START

Stream near Sopley.

100 yards, cross a stream and in a few yards look for another fingerpost tucked behind the hedge on the right. Here go straight ahead (west) along a farm track for three-quarters of a mile to meet the Avon Valley Path at a single oak tree. Turn left here on the Avon Valley Path and follow the green AVP signs back to Sopley.

Four-mile walk. Having crossed straight over the Ripley road, follow the track ahead past a cottage which has one of the last surviving traditional local cottage gardens. Cross a bridge and turn left, going southwards along the western bank of the stream and on the field boundary for another 600 yards until the path crosses a second lane to join the AVP. This leads southwards back to Sopley.

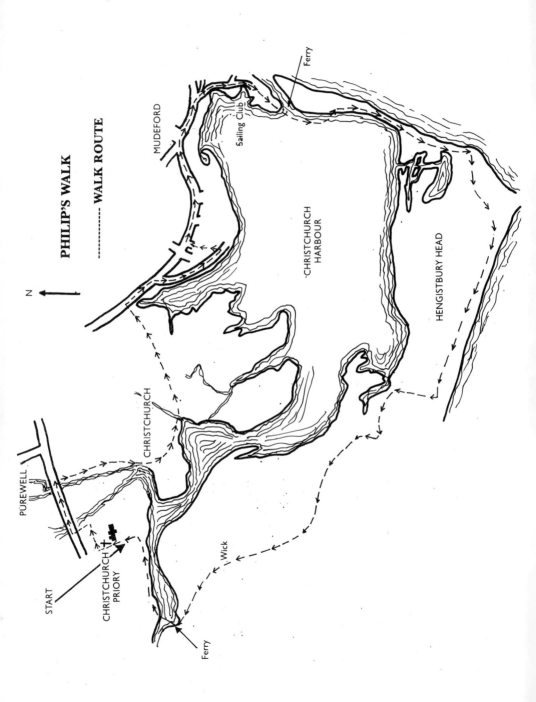

PHILIP'S WALK

------- WALK ROUTE

N

MUDEFORD

Ferry

Sailing Club

CHRISTCHURCH HARBOUR

HENGISTBURY HEAD

PUREWELL

CHRISTCHURCH

START

CHRISTCHURCH PRIORY

Wick

Ferry

PHILIP'S WALK — A CIRCULAR FROM CHRISTCHURCH
5 miles

Christchurch can be reached by bus or train from several directions but note that the Ringwood to Christchurch bus does not run on Sundays.

There are several car parks in the town — one adjacent to the Priory, which is the starting point for the walk.

This walk commences from the end of the Avon Valley Path and passes through some interesting parts of old Christchurch. There are views of Hengistbury Head from Stanpit Marshes; the Isle of Wight is visible from Mudeford Sandspit and from the Head the panorama of the Harbour, the Priory and St. Catherine's Hill can be seen.

Note that this walk involves using two ferries (for which there are charges) and that they only run from Easter until the end of October.

The Route

Start at Christchurch Priory (GR 160925) facing the North Porch which is the main entrance. Turn left (east) and walk along the length of the Priory to a low wall at its end. Turn right (south) and walk through a wooded patch to a garden. On the left-hand side, towards the Mill Stream, is the Garde Robe, which is a medieval 'loo'.

At the entrance to the garden turn right and walk along the metalled footpath keeping the old stone wall on the right. Go through the opened wrought iron gates. The building in front is known as Place Mill and is mentioned in the Doomsday Book. Turn left, go over the bridge, then turn left again and walk along the Convent Walk (east) with the Mill Stream to the left. Go over the millstream race, through an arch and the River Avon is straight ahead. Turn left and walk between the Millstream and the River. On the left-hand side of the Millstream is the Constable's House which was part of the Norman Castle and has one of the first chimneys to be built in England.

Cross the road, turn right and walk for about a quarter of a mile (east) to go over the second bridge. Across the road are the railings separating the public slipway with the gable end of the building beyond. Make for the right (west) side of this building, turn left and cross a green sward to a car park. Turn right (south), walk to the end of the car park, cross a road and go between the steel gate and a ditch. Continue with the bank on the left and ditch on the right for about 300 yards to a gate in the bank. Turn right, cross the stile and duckboards and about ten yards from the river turn left, keeping the river on the right for about 200 yards until it bends to the right. Here turn left away from the river.

Facing Hegistbury Head, look for a duckboard about ten yards into the marsh. Cross this and subsequent duckboards aiming towards the Coastguard Station on the Head. Eventually cross a small bridge over a drainage ditch after which the duckboards bear to the left (east), right (south-east) then left again (east) to reach a stile. Cross this, a footbridge and another stile, then walk in the same direction until coming to the main track. Turn left and walk north-easterly for about half a mile. The track narrows to about three feet between bushes, but carry on through a kissing gate then follow the right-hand path to its end. Turn right (south-west) and cross the recreation ground towards some white houses for about a quarter of a mile to reach a hedge. Turn left (north-east) with the hedge on the right and after about 200 yards go to the right of a black and white building and through the car park beyond the road. Turn right (south-east) for about 250 yards, passing the Guide Hut on the right, to a gap between houses and a footpath sign. Turn right and follow the footpath along Fishermen's Bank (where Fishermen used to draw up their nets to dry).

Carry on in the same direction (south of south-west) over the public highway, between white posts and follow the concrete fence. This turns several times. At the end of a lean-to garage, turn right, then left up the metalled track and follow this to the highway which leads to the main road. Here turn right for about 880 yards, passing 'The Nelson Tavern' and the 'The Avonmouth Hotel'. At a telephone box turn right down a minor road to its junction with a more substantial road. Here turn right, cross the bridge over a little stream and take the footpath which leads down to the harbour. Go along the footpath adjacent to the harbour but at a junction of paths take the left-hand footpath to reach the road. Turn right, walk towards buildings and go between the 'Haven House Inn' and the Highcliffe Sailing club. Pass between the white Fishermen's Shop and the Dutch cottages and head towards the sea. At the railings turn right along the quay to reach and take the ferry which crosses 'The Run' to reach Mudeford Sandspit.

Having crossed, go towards the beach huts, turn right at the harbourside beach and walk along the sand (generally south-west) to reach a gravel track. Continue on a metalled road, but when this turns right, away from the huts, take the sandy track to the left. Cross another metal road to reach steps which ascend the hill. There are exceptional views of the Isle of Wight on the left.

The steps lead up onto Hengistbury Head, which was an Iron Age Hill Fort. At the top take the right-hand path leading towards the Coastguard Station. There are marvellous views of the Harbour, Priory and, beyond, St. Catherine's Hill.

The river Avon at Christchurch.
Below: The Norman built Constable's House at Christchurch.

On reaching the Coastguard Station, follow the track to the trig point and turn left down the hill. When the track forks, take the path on the right and at the bottom of the hill turn right. At a metalled road turn left and walk along towards a thatched building (Warden's cottage and Council depot). Just before the building take a gravelled footpath on the right, through bushes, and at its junction with the road, turn right to the DCC Outdoor Studies Centre. Left of the entrance is a sign indicating the way to Wick Village. Go through the kissing gate and along the grassy track through Wick Fields (generally north-west) for just under a mile. Go through a kissing gate beside the reed beds and continue with the Priory ahead. Cross the wooden bridge to reach and follow a gravel path. Go through a steel-barred kissing gate, take the right-hand fork in the path and walk along the gravel path through bramble bushes to an open field. Here take the grassy track nearest the river and continue, first to the right then left and through another steel-barred kissing gate. Take the path to the river, turn left and walk first alongside it then through bushes and out to an open space. Follow the right-hand gravel track to the landing stage for the Wick Ferry which must be taken across the water.

Once across, go up the steps and over the paved area towards the road. About five yards from the road, go through the gap in the wall to the right and follow the path along the river. At the Quay turn left and walk up the little cobbled road with the Old Mill Tea Rooms on the left and Place Mill on the right. Just before the Priory Gardens, go through a gap in the wall on the left, cross the car park and in a few yards turn right into the Priory Grounds.

Acknowledgements
The following members of the Ramblers' Association are thanked for their contributions to this book:

Walk descriptions	Photographs
Derek Allen	
Erica and John Bamford	John Bamford
Anne and Trevor Davies	Trevor Davies
Marjorie and Jim Kerr	Marjorie Kerr
Ernest Paine	Thelma Paine
Cliff Roffey	Vic Ruston
Vic Ruston	
Philip Samuel	

For further information about the Ramblers' Association contact: Ramblers' Association, 1-5 Wandsworth Road, London SW8 2XX.

COVER: The cover was designed by ROBIN PELLING.

Also by the New Forest Ramblers' Association:

Walks in the New Forest

Further countryside books for your enjoyment:

Walks in conjunction with Hampshire Ramblers' Association or associated group:

'Walks in Mid-Hampshire'
by Brenda M. Parker.

'Walks in North-East Hampshire'

'Walks in East Hampshire'
by Brenda Parker

New edition with updated walks.

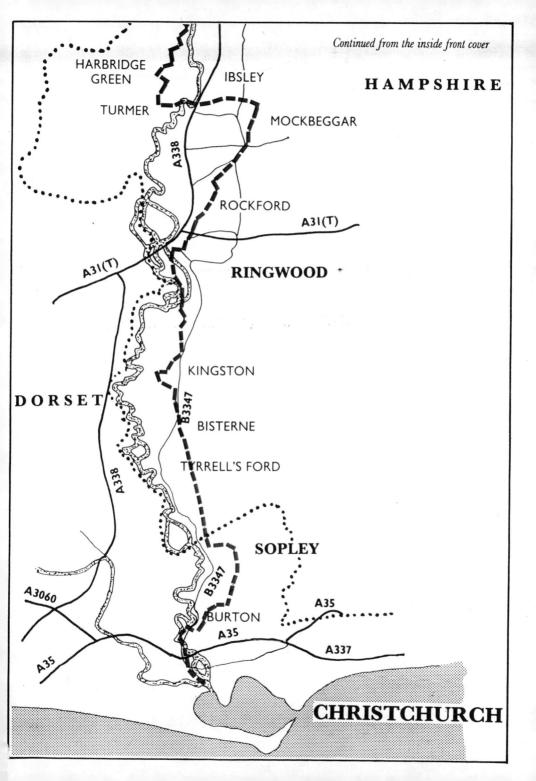

Continued from the inside front cover

HARBRIDGE GREEN

IBSLEY

HAMPSHIRE

TURMER

MOCKBEGGAR

A338

ROCKFORD

A31(T)

A31(T)

RINGWOOD

KINGSTON

B3347

DORSET

BISTERNE

TYRRELL'S FORD

A338

SOPLEY

B3347

A3060

A35

BURTON

A35

A35

A337

CHRISTCHURCH